Hello!
I am a penguin.

Penguins are excellent swimmers. They spend most of their lives in the water.

Penguins are expert divers. Some can dive as deep as 1800 feet (550 m).

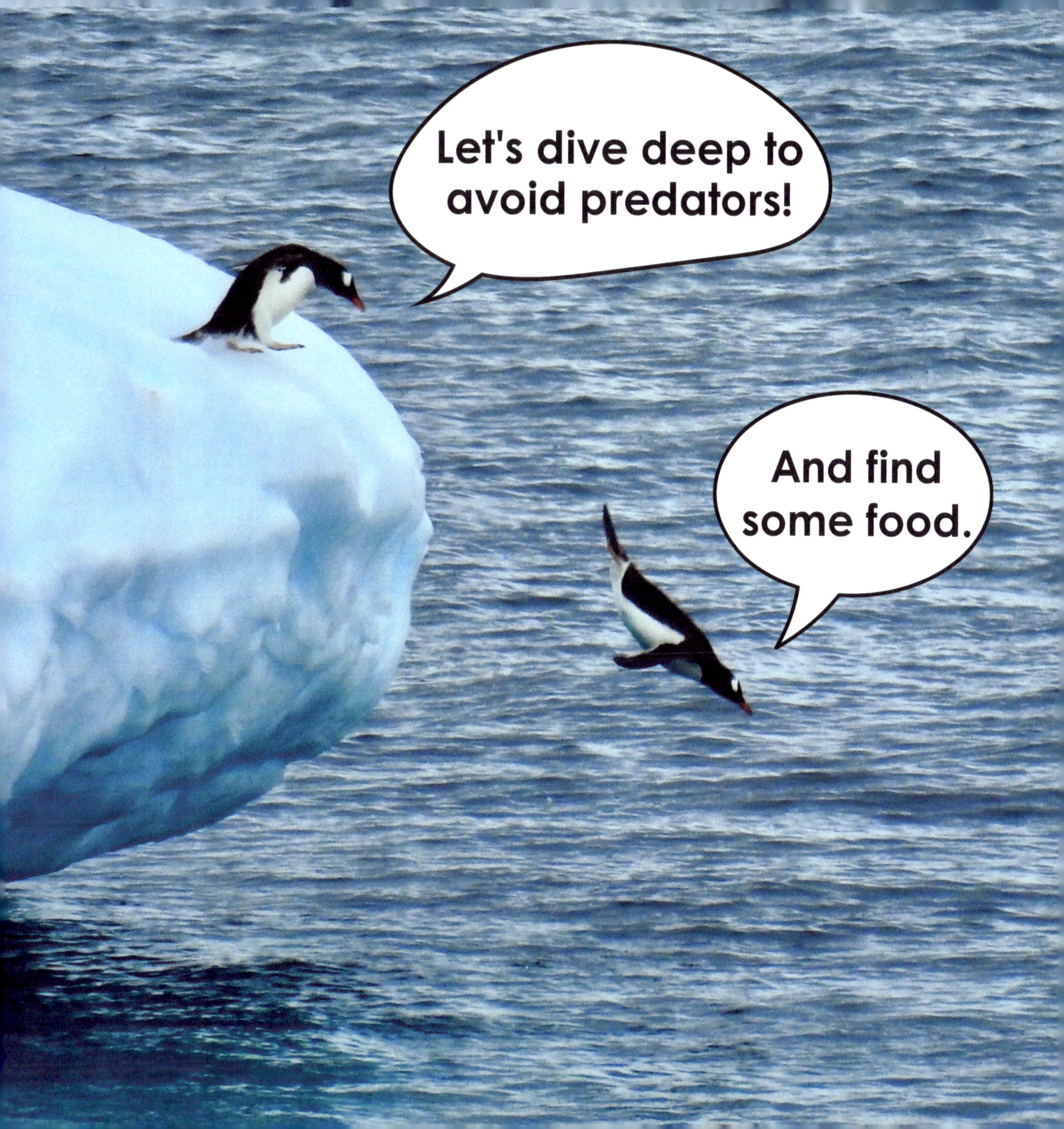
Let's dive deep to avoid predators!
And find some food.

Penguins have webbed feet that work like flippers.

While penguins are great swimmers, they aren't so good at walking (or running).

Penguins' black and white feathers make them hard to spot for predators.

From the bottom, we blend in with the light sky.

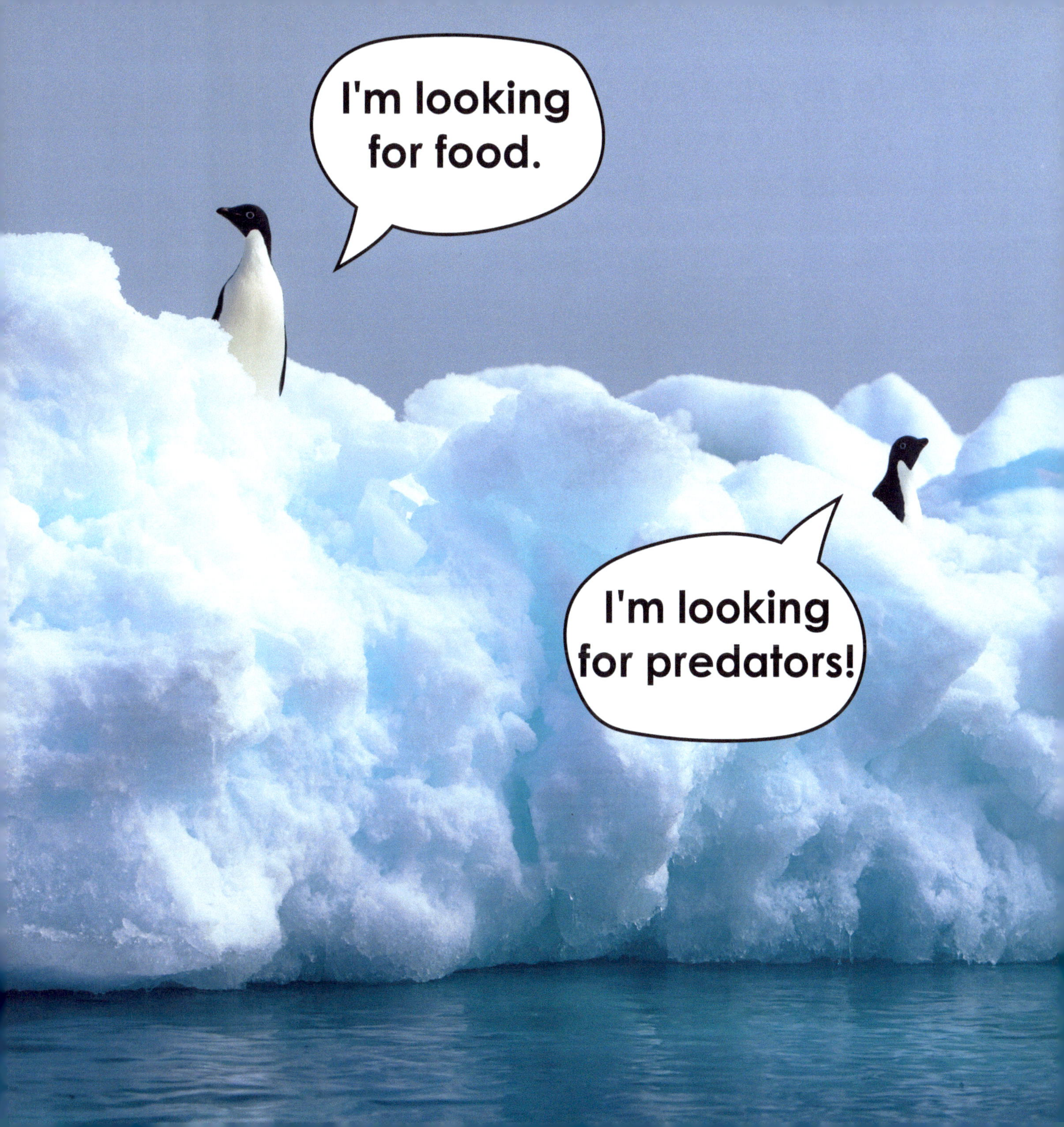
I'm looking for food.
I'm looking for predators!

When molting, penguins can't hunt or swim. So, they gather in groups during this time.

Penguins have only one mate for life. Once they find their partner, they stay together and raise chicks together.

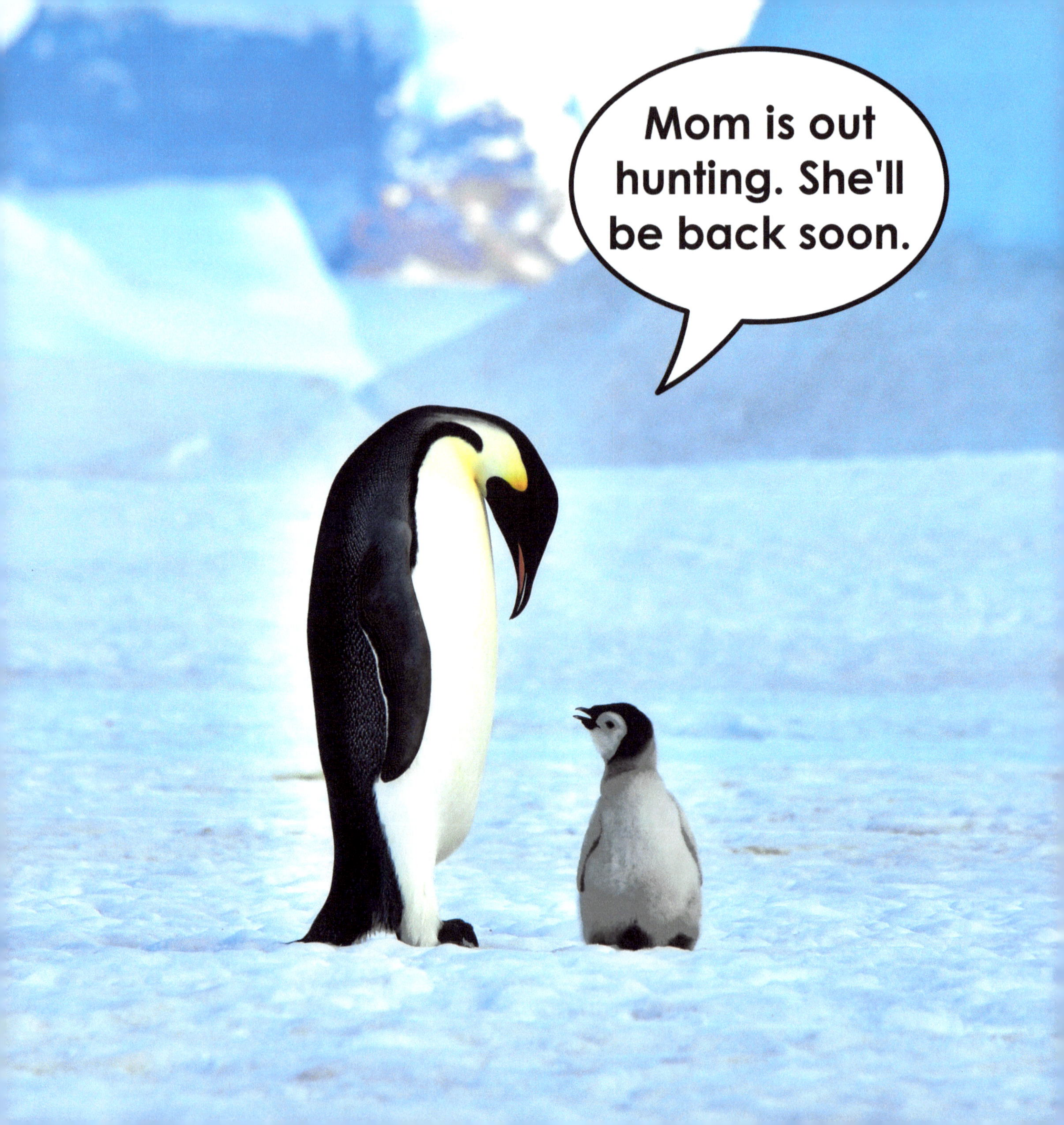
Mom is out hunting. She'll be back soon.

Penguins are excellent parents. The male and female work as a team to take care of their eggs and chicks.

Penguins huddle together to stay warm. This is called a "crèche".

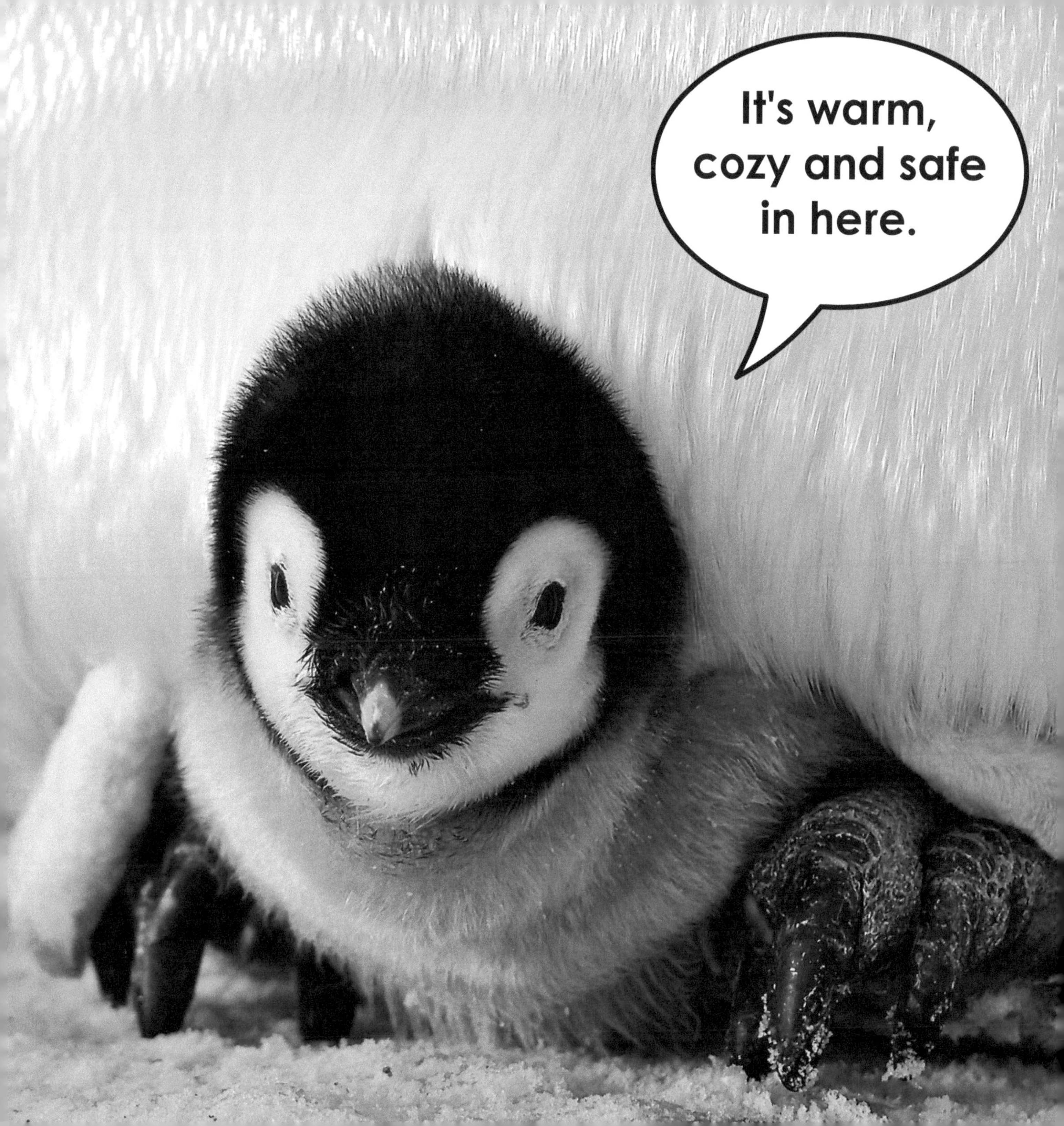
It's warm, cozy and safe in here.

Some penguins make their nests out of rocks. They're called "rockeries".

A rockery is a safe and secure place for my eggs.
This nest ROCKS!

A group of penguins is called a "colony".

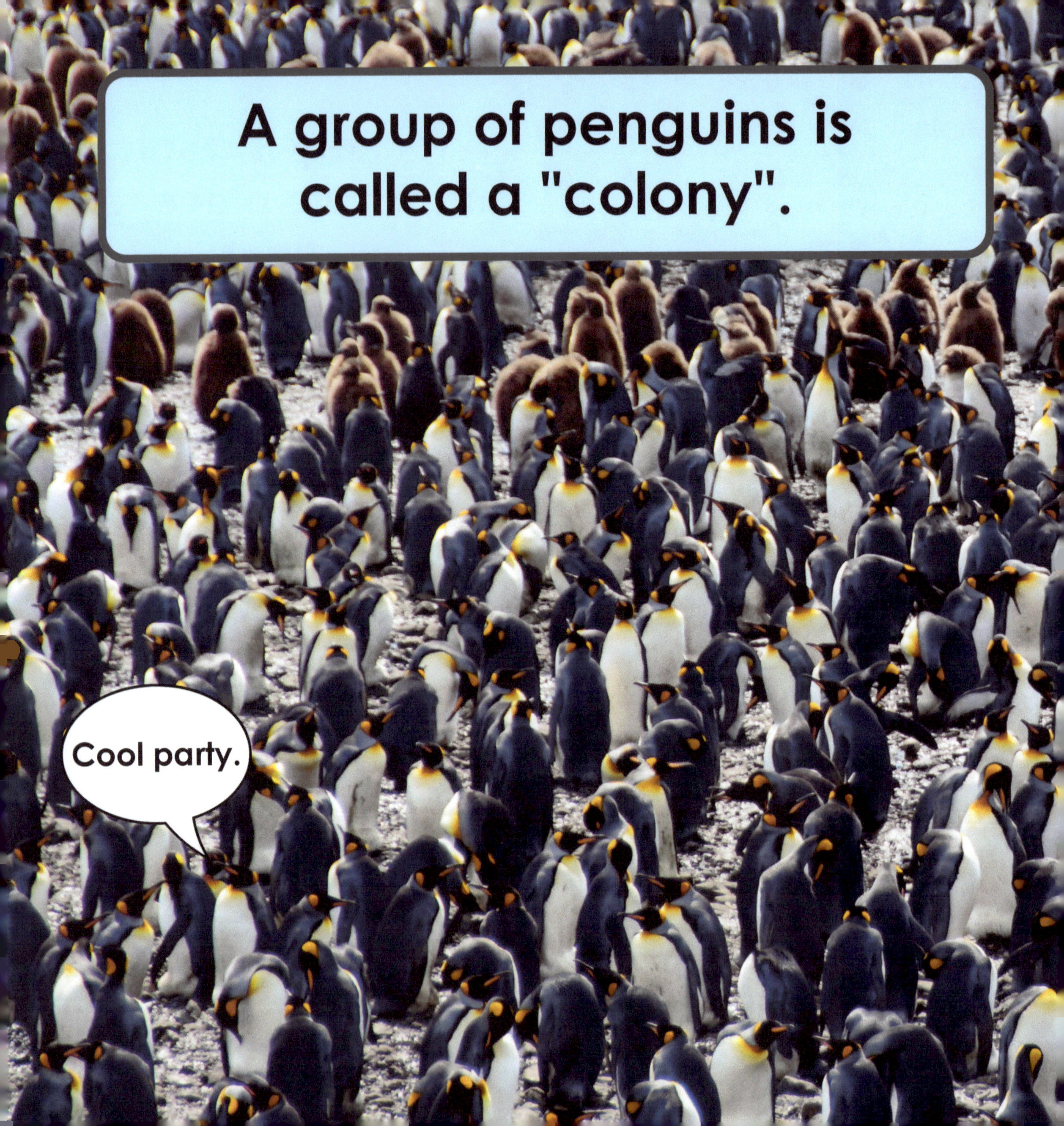

Some penguin colonies have thousands or even millions of penguins.

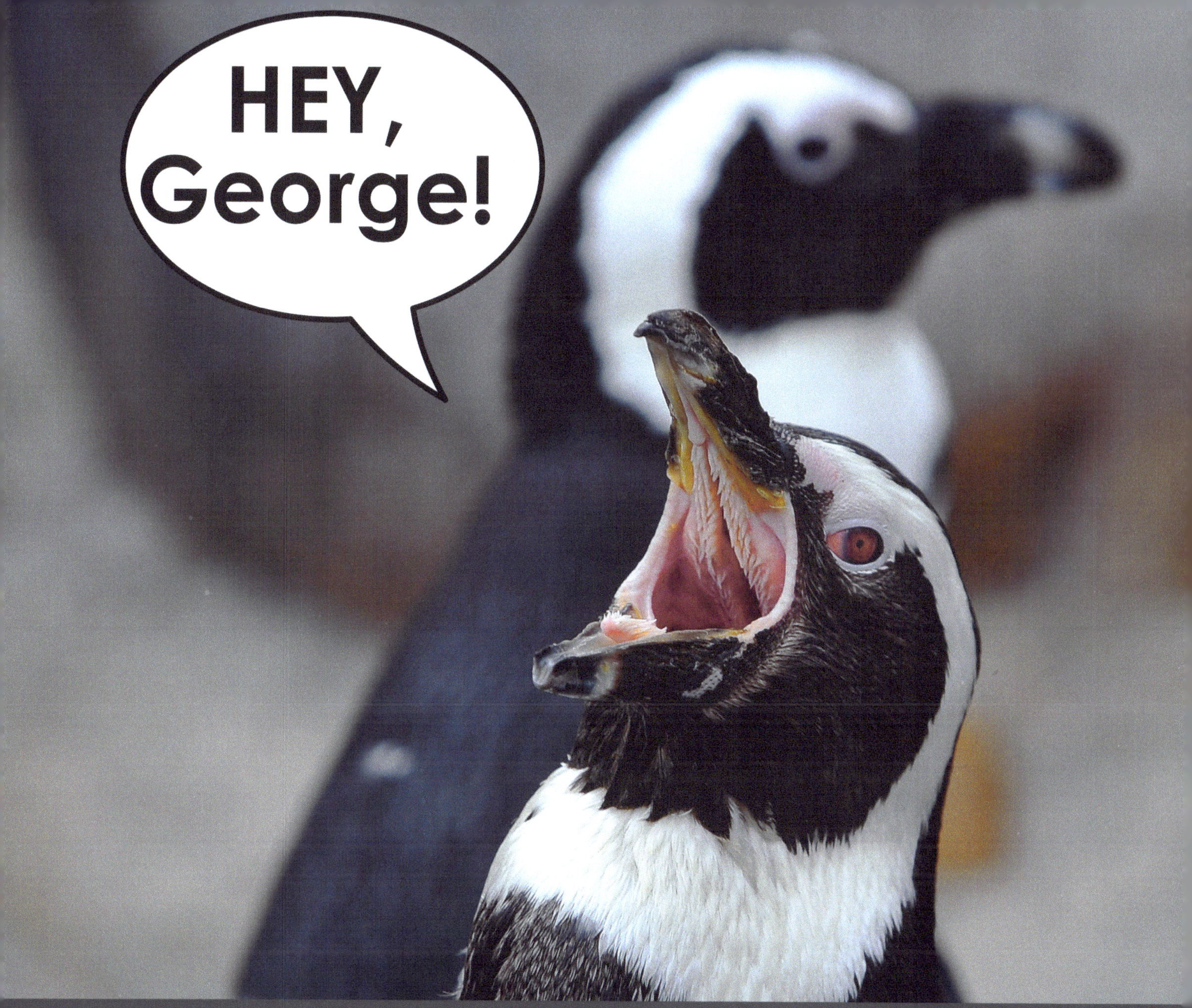

They also make special calls to recognize their friends.

Penguins make strong friendships with others in their colony.

Penguin friendships are built on trust, cooperation, and mutual support.

Here I come.

Friends in a penguin colony often engage in activities like sliding on ice together, playing tag, or synchronized swimming.

Hello parents!

Visit us to find out about new releases and *FREE* offers. We'll let you know when we have a new release coming out and how you can get it for FREE.

And you can cast your vote for what book we make next!

scan here

ActiveBrainsBooks.com

or visit here

---

scan here

Let us know what you think. As an independent publisher, your honest reviews mean a lot to us and our business. We'd love to hear from you!

amazon.com/review/create-review/

or visit here

FOLLOW US on Amazon.

amazon.com/author/activebrainsbooks

ActiveBrainsBooks.com

ACTIVE BRAINS